SCHIRMER'S LIBRARY
OF MUSICAL CLASSICS

Vol. 2137

10 ESSENTIAL PIANO SONATAS

Beethoven, Haydn, Mozart, Schubert

ISBN 978-1-5400-2476-3

G. SCHIRMER, *Inc.*

DISTRIBUTED BY

HAL•LEONARD®

7777 W. BLUEMOUND RD. P.O. BOX 13819 MILWAUKEE, WI 53213

www.musicsalesclassical.com
www.halleonard.com

CONTENTS

to Joseph Haydn

PIANO SONATA NO. 1
in F minor

Edited and with fingering by
Hans von Bülow
and Sigmund Lebert

Ludwig van Beethoven
Op. 2, No. 1

Abbreviations:* M. T. signifies Main Theme; S. T., Sub-Theme; Cl. T., Closing Theme; D. G., Development- group; R., Return; Tr., Transition; Md. T., Mid-Theme; Ep., Episode.

* German equivalents: M.T. Hauptsatz, S.T. Seitensatz; Cl. T. Schlusssatz, D.G. Durchführungssatz, R. Rückgang, **Tr.** Übergang, Md. T. Mittelsatz, Ep. Zwischensatz, Coda. Anhang.

a) easier:

Adagio ($\flat$ = 88.)

a)   b) The left-hand part kept subordinate, though the sustained bass notes, in contrast to the 16ths, should be somewhat emphasized.

c)   d)   e)   f)   g)

a)

a)

Menuetto
Allegretto (♩ = 63)

Trio

Men. D. C.

a) In this theme *Piano* and *Forte* are to be sharply contradistinguished, without gradual transition from one to the other.

a) In this accompaniment the left hand must be subordinated to the melody.

a)

a) The left hand, having the melody, must play somewhat louder than the right, both here and on the repetition.

to Countess von Browne

PIANO SONATA NO. 5
in C minor

Edited and with fingering by
Hans von Bülow
and Sigmund Lebert

Ludwig van Beethoven
Op. 10, No. 1

Abbreviations: M.T. signifies Main Theme; S.T., Sub-Theme; Cl.T., Closing Theme; D.G., Development-group; R., Return; Tr., Transition; Md.T., Mid-Theme; Ep., Episode.

Allegro molto e con brio. (♩·=69.)

a) The term *rinforzando* (reinforcing), though primarily referring, like *sforzando*, to a single note, may also have a more general scope; as in this case, where the dotted quarter-notes are to be struck *sforzando* (and with decidedly more force than in the parallel measures preceding); but the entire 4-measure passage, as well, is to be played in a moderate *forte*.

b) Take care to give these rests, and others that follow, their full value.

a)

a)

a)

b) Bring out finely the part having the melody; in the third measure, in particular, the lower part in the right hand and the higher part in the left must be subordinated.

c) Execute this arpeggio by sounding the tones in rapid succession, from the lowest bass tone to the highest treble tone, and with a *crescendo,* so that the final tone is struck most forcibly.

d)

a) In these three measures the tenor, and in the third the alto as well, must be brought out as a melodic part, though subordinate to the soprano.

b) Play these groups of unaccented grace-notes within the time-value of the fourth sixteenth-note of their respective measures.

c) Play the melody with a certain stress, but very delicately.   **d)**

e) These groups of 12 and 6 64th- notes are to be considered, like the succeeding ones, as respectively fourfold and double triplets of 64ths.

f)

a) *Rinforzando* signifies here, and in what follows, simply a higher degree of power on the whole.

c) As on p.25, c).

b)

or easier:

a) As on p. 26, a).
b) As on p. 26, c).

a) Make the highest part most prominent, the bass less so, and the inner parts least of all.

b)

c) Here the higher part in the left hand must be brought out parallel with, yet subordinate to, the treble melody; the lower right-hand part should be most subdued, except in the passage in the next measure, which must be duly emphasized.

d) The inner part in the right hand must sound as the principal melody in this measure.

Finale.

Prestissimo. ($\circ$ = 100.)

a) or easier: b) or easier:

c) The dots added by Beethoven to these soprano notes signify (as is sometimes also the case with the older composers) not so much *staccato* as *sforzando*.

d) The right hand must begin together with the left, and reach the highest tone simultaneously with the latter.

a) Do not retard.   b) To be held very long.

a) *(musical notation)*

b) Both the *calando* (here used in its proper sense as equivalent to *decrescendo*) and more especially the *ritardando* must be commenced here very cautiously, so that the intensification of both may be effected very gradually up to the measure marked *pp* and *Adagio*.

c) These appoggiaturas are to be played with moderate rapidity, without robbing the following dotted quarter-note of any of its time-value, which must be still longer than that of the preceding G♭.

d) These appoggiaturas are likewise unaccented (*auftakt*-notes), so that the eighth-note G retains its full value.

to Prince Carl von Lichnowky

PIANO SONATA NO. 8

Edited and with fingering by
Hans von Bülow
and Sigmund Lebert

in C minor
"Pathétique"

Ludwig van Beethoven
Op. 13

Abbreviations: M. T. signifies Main Theme; S. T., Sub-Theme; Cl. T., Closing Theme; D. G., Development-group; R., Return; Tr., Transition; Md. T., Mid-Theme; Ep., Episode.

a) The 32nd-note must be perceptibly detached from the next-following dotted sixteenth-note, and this latter sustained for its full value — a mode of execution peculiar to such rhythms in the old masters; compare Händel's Prelude to the F-minor Fugue, and Bach's Prelude to the G-minor Fugue in Part II of "The Well-tempered Clavichord."

b) This run should be performed expressively, and in the second half with a slight retardation, so as to bring out the melodic outlines.

c) Carefully observe the increasing value of the "lifting-note;" the first time, the sixth eighth in the measure is only a sixteenth-note; in the next measure, the D on the second eighth is a full eighth-note, while the F on the sixth eighth becomes a quarter-note. This effects a melodic intensification.

Allegro di molto e con brio. (♩=144.)

a) The relation between the movement of the *Introduction* and the *Allegro* is properly this: That a whole note in the latter is exactly equivalent to an eighth-note in the former. Consequently, the *Allegro* may be begun at the rate of M.M. ♩=132, which movement would not, however, be fast enough further on, in view of the passionate character developed.

b) In tremolo-figures like these, the player should be content to mark only such bass notes (and then only at the first stroke) as indicate a new progression in the harmony.

c) The direction *agitato* also calls for a *non legato* as strict as possible, which, of course, must not impair the evenness of the movement.

a) Although this *"second"* subject, too, is passionately agitated, the unvarying tempestuous sweep of the first cannot be kept up throughout. Play the first measure of each four-measure period—the preluding bass—somewhat more quietly, the following three with all the more animation; shade the 16 measures in Eb-minor differently from the parallel passage in Db-major; in short, invest the entire dialogue with the most varied coloring possible.

b) Execution: according to the familiar rule, that all graces take their value from, and are played within, the value of the principal note.

c) Execution: according to the same rule; beware of the facile and tasteless triplet in eighth-notes, to which even the anticipated passing shake would be preferable, though against the rules.

a) These first 4 measures are to be played without the least retardation, yet very quietly, and with no accentuation of the accompaniment.

a) The hold (pause) must be sustained precisely 3 measures, so as to form another 4-measure period.

But a quarter-rest should precede the reprise of the first division:

b) Retard the entrance of the B in the bass, in order to enhance the pleasurable suspense attendant upon the enharmonic change of the diminished chord of the seventh in the transition from G-minor to E-minor; and play the following passage throughout with full dreamy freedom.

Allegro molto e con brio.

a) Despite the identity of this phrase with that in meas. 5 of the first *Grave*, it must now be played with a wholly different expression — or, rather, with none whatever, this being rendered necessary by the doubled rapidity of the movement (♪ in the *Grave* = 𝅝 in the *Allegro*).

b) Although the phrasing 𝄞𝅗𝅥𝅘𝅥𝅮 etc. would more nearly correspond to the original form of this passage in meas. 7 *et seq.* of the so-called second subject (Eb-minor), it would not be in keeping with the general (progressional) character of the development-section.

c) The player should slightly sustain the several tones 𝄢𝅘𝅥 but not so as to make the movement heavy.

a) As an exception to the rule, this trill must not begin on the auxiliary, so as not to blur the melodic

outlines; seven notes 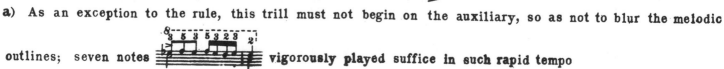 vigorously played suffice in such rapid tempo

a) This *piano* must enter abruptly, which requires some practice, especially with the left hand; similarly in the parallel passage 4 measures further on.

a) In the original the *decrescendo* begins at this measure, which seems to us rather too prolonged for 6 full measures, — the more so, because an actual *forte* would be inadmissible in the preceding; for this reason we consider a *poco cresc.* more suitable for the first two measures.

b) Take care not to play E♭ instead of F in the right hand, as a C-minor chord is out of the question here; the C in both Soprano and Bass is simply a passing-note of the dominant chord.

a) Sustain the hold (pause) 3 full measures (comp. {Note a, the first holds in the *Grave* have precisely the same dura-
{Page 118); tion (subtracting the 32nd-note).

b) The bass note on the third fourth-note must have a penetrating and prolonged tone, in order to be quite audible
through the seventh eighth-note as the root of the chord of the sixth.

c) This coda cannot be played too rapidly.

d) It is best not to use the pedal with these chords.

Adagio cantabile. (♪ = 60)

a) To the best of our knowledge no one has yet remarked the striking affinity of the theme of this movement, even with reference to its external melodic structure, to that of one of the loftiest *Adagios* of grandest scope from the Master's last period; — we mean the *Adagio* of the Ninth Symphony, written almost a quarter of a century later. The performance of both demands an equally inspired mood. The player's task, to "make his fingers sing," may perhaps necessitate a more frequent use of the pedal than we have indicated, which must of course be controlled by a most watchful ear.

b) This first middle section of the Rondo (for such this *Adagio* is in form) may be taken slightly *meno andante*, i. e., slower; but no more so than needful (so as not to drag), and, therefore, in only a few places.

c) The turns in this and the next measure should not commence with, but immediately after, a sixteenth-note in the bass, thus: and:

a) A tasteful execution of this grace is impossible in strict time. An abbreviation of the first two principal notes (C and B♭) being quite as impracticable as a shifting of the inverted mordent into the preceding measure as an unaccented appoggiatura, the measure must simply be extended by an additional 32nd-note.

b) In this repetition of the theme, the left hand may be allowed to play a more expressive part; and, on the whole, a somewhat lighter shading of the melody is now admissible by way of contrast to the following (gloomier) middle section.

c) The ascending diminished fifth may be phrased, as it were, like a question, to which the succeeding bass figure may be regarded as the answer.

a) It appears advisable slightly to hasten this measure and the next, and then to retard the third not inconsiderably; the former on account of the cessation in the harmonic advance, the latter by reason of the varied modulation, which must be quite free from disquieting haste in its return to the theme.

b) Though strictly subordinated to the melody, the triplets should be brought out with animated distinctness.

c) The two 32nd-notes in the melody may very properly be sounded with the last note of the triplet of 16th-notes in the accompaniment; whereas a mathematically exact division would probably confuse both parts.

a) Execute like a triplet:

b) In the original, the shading of this passage is marked differently from that two measures before, the *diminuendo* already beginning with C, and not with A♭ as here marked. This latter nuance – the prolongation of the *crescendo* – appeals to our feeling as the more delicate, "more tenderly passionate," to quote Richard Wagner's happy remark on the "Interpretation of Beethoven."

c) Mark the separation of the slurs in this figure and those following; the six notes sound trivial if slurred together.

Rondo.

Allegro. ($\sf d$=96.)

a) Although this third movement is less "pathetic" than the preceding ones, the player alone will be to blame should the Pathetic Sonata end apathetically. The original, to be sure, contains only the most indispensable expression-marks, which it has been the aim of our Edition to supplement efficiently; as, for example, by the *crescendo* ending *piano* in measures 2-3, by emphasizing the distinction to be made, in the figures for the left hand, between the parts (tones) which are essential (independent) organic elements, and those which are mere harmonic filling; etc.

b) In executing this grace, the player must be careful not to produce the effect of parallel octaves with the bass (F-A♭, and in the next measure E♭-G); rather than this, the slide might be treated as an appendage to the fore-going notes.

a) There can hardly be a doubt that the Master was compelled, by the restricted compass of the keyboard of his day (only up to F³), to content himself with the fifth of the dominant chord, instead of rising to the higher seventh (A♭) as in the three other parallel passages. A change in conformity with his original intention is impracticable, however, because the ensuing measure would then be made to lie an octave higher, and would sound somewhat thin for the first time (it is immediately repeated in the octave).

b) These imitations, although *piano,* must be played with great animation, and not in that characterless *legato* which might be called anti-symphonic.

c) The preceding Remark applies equally to this and similar passages.

a) The fingering given by us serves to aid in executing this run with the exact rhythmic divisions desired by the composer. The hold which follows appears really superfluous; for, by the prolongation of the chord through $1\frac{1}{4}$ measures, all demands of the pulsing rhythm ____ which goes on even during the rests of a piece ____ are fully met.

Tranquillo. a)

a) The tempo, of course, remains the same, but free from any fluctuating agitation. Observe, that the theme "proper" begins with an ascending fourth, consequently, the left hand should be slightly emphasized in the fifth and sixth measures. This holds good for meas. 13, 14, etc.

b) The mark **ff** is set rather early, in view of the fact, that the intensification continues through the next six measures. For this reason, the player will do well to husband his strength at first.

11611

a) The more tempestuously the 12 preceding measures have been played, the longer may this hold (see Note a, page 160) be sustained.

a) The second subject must be played more delicately and quietly here than at its first entrance in Eb major.

b) A collision of the two parts on D^2 must be avoided by anticipating the right hand by an arpeggio in the left, lifting the left-hand thumb instantly after the stroke; thus:

c) The second note in the bass might, in conformity with the parallel passages in the first division, be Ab.

a) These next **13** measures should be played with considerable freedom as regards tempo, and with a decided independent stress on the lower part in the left hand. Special attention should be paid to the composer's directions concerning both the shading of meas. **6-7** and **8-9**, and their phrasing, which is not in one-measure rhythm (as the motive at the first glance apparently invites), but in two-measure rhythm. In proportion to the greater or lesser degree of passion put forth by the player before the *calando*, this latter is to be conceived as a *diminuendo* and *ritardando*. Excess in either direction is, of course, reprehensible.

b) Particularly note the *Auftakt* (fractional initial measure) in the bass, here representing the regular introduction . By playing the theme wholly without shading on its fourth (and last) appearance, the close is well prepared and led up to.

a) Moderate the tempo on commencing this measure, in order that the ensuing run can be executed precisely according to the given divisions and without the least retardation. The following hold may be sustained very long—as long as the sonority of the piano permits.

b) A *ritardando* in this epilogue would be in bad taste; the tempo must be strictly sustained to the close.

c) The *fff* is found in all the old Editions,—almost the sole instance where this superlative, surely as frequently intended as rarely used is employed by the Master. Hence follows the necessity of an unusually powerful *crescendo* in the preceding run.

to Countess Julia Guicciardi

PIANO SONATA NO. 14
in C-sharp minor
"Moonlight"

Edited and with fingering by
Hans von Bülow
and Sigmund Lebert

Ludwig van Beethoven
Op. 27, No. 2

Abbreviations: M. T. signifies Main Theme; S. T., Sub-Theme; Cl. T., Closing Theme; D. G., Development-group; R., Return; Tr., Transition; Md. T., Mid-Theme; Ep., Episode.

a) It is evident that the highest part, as the melody, requires a firmer touch than the accompanying triplet-figure; and the first note in the latter must never produce the effect of a doubling of the melody in the lower octave.

b) A more frequent use of the pedal than is marked by the editor, and limited here to the most essential passages, is allowable; it is not advisable, however, to take the original directions *sempre senza sordini* (i. e., without dampers) too literally.

a) The player must guard against carrying his hand back with over-anxious haste. For, in any event, a strict pedantic observance of time is out of place in this period, which has rather the character of an improvisation.

a) The notes with a dash above them may properly be dwelt upon in such a way as to give them the effect of suspensions, e. g.,   : in fact, a utilization of the inner parts, in accordance   with the laws of euphony and the course of the modulation, is recommended throughout the piece.

II. Allegretto.a) (♩ = 56.)

a) *Allegretto* means *poco allegro*. The movement should not exceed a moderate minuet-tempo, in this point precisely resembling the analogous movements in the Sonatas Op. 2, Nos 1 and 2; Op. 10, No 2; Op. 14, No 1, not to speak of later ones. This anti-Scherzo is, indeed, a lyrical Intermezzo between two tragical Nocturnes. Franz Liszt's clever *mot*: "*Une fleur entre deux abîmes*" (a flower betwixt two abysses) gives the key to the true interpretation.

b) Special care must be bestowed on the twofold task of the right hand — a songful leading of the melody, with a light and graceful *staccato* in the second part, which latter combines with the left-hand part as a third factor.

a) A very common amateurish error — which, we regret to say, is countenanced here and in other places by Herr Lebert's otherwise so meritorious edition — is the notion that a closer *legato* is obtainable,
in descending octave-passages, by a change of fingers. Precisely the opposite effect is produced by the
following manipulation: ; the higher part, the one most strongly affecting the ear, suffers a most
sensible interruption. A slight muscular stretching of the palm of the hand, which is no harder to learn
than shifting on a stringed instrument, will amply fulfil all requirements.

b) An undelayed attack (of the Finale) is quite as indispensable to the general effect as in the two repris-
es preceding.

III. Presto agitato. (♩=88.)

a) This passage, up to the abrupt stroke on the fourth beat in measure 2, must be played with almost ethereal lightness in the very smoothest *piano*, and (if only for the sake of distinctness) as little *legato* as is in any way compatible with the great rapidity of the movement.

b) The second stroke has only the significance of an echo, the repercussion of the first. In measure 8 it is different, owing to its leading over to new matter.

a) This grace is written out in conformity with its undeviating mode of execution. Avoid a repeated accentuation of the lowest bass note; an accent is needful only on its first entrance.

b) The rapid movement, conjoined with required exertion of strength, hardly admits of a longer trill

than: (or:).

a) These thirds can be brought out with perfect distinctness only by means of this fingering, troublesome though it be.

b) It is self-evident that a hammering-out of these "passionate" eighth-notes in strict time would be incorrect in an æsthetic sense. By playing the first half of the measure with stronger emphasis (and hence greater freedom), as is demanded in particular by the peculiar rhythmic importance of the second eighth-note, and somewhat accelerating the second half, both the unity of the measure as such, and also the psychical agitation, receive due consideration. **c)** This melodic phrase, whose performance demands the intensest feeling, is probably to be understood

thus: i.e., more singingly sustained than the marking denotes.

a) The literal execution is: ![figure]

b) The repetition prescribed here according to custom impresses us as a chilling tautology.

c) This movement-figure, like the similar one in the right hand 4 measures further on, must be played entirely without accentuation; only in the principal modulations, e. g., the transition from F#-minor to G-major and back, individual characteristic intervals may be slightly emphasized. On the other hand, a transformation of the figures into an indistinct *tremolo* would, of course, be wholly out of place.

a) In the analogous passage in the first division, this period embraces 4 measures, whereas it has but 3 here. There is no reason why either should be altered for the sake of symmetry of pattern. Both are good, and greater brevity and conciseness in form are æsthetically justified in repetitions.

CODA.
animato.

Tempo I.

a) This second hold (*pause*) may be sustained longer than the preceding. Further, a slight rest must intervene (for acoustic reasons, apart from aesthetic ones) before the reentrance of the first subject, as is indicated by a ⌢ over the bar.

a) There is no irreverence, even to the letter of the composer's work, in enhancing — in analogy with the D-minor Sonata Op. 31 Nº 2 — the accent marked on the fourth beat by a chord struck with the left hand.

Tempo I, ma tranquillo.

Adagio. **b)**

a) The editor performs this cadenza with the following rhythmic divisions, the required *ritardando* then result-

ing as a matter of course:

b) *Adagio*: twice as slow as the *Presto* - movement, but not slower.

c) Avoid a *crescendo* in the preceding measures; the *forte* must enter with instantaneous abruptness, giving us
a reproduction of the principal divisions in miniature — the deep melancholy of the *Adagio*, the wild desne
ration of the *Finale*.

to Magdalene von Kurzbeck

PIANO SONATA
in E-flat Major

Based on the original text
edited by Karl Päsler

Franz Joseph Haydn
Hob. XVI:52

a) = 〰

Adagio

Finale
Presto

a) *ad libitum*

PIANO SONATA
in C Major

Edited, revised and fingered by
Richard Epstein

Wolfgang Amadeus Mozart
K. 309

Allegro con spirito (♩=144)

a) and b) A short trill, commencing on the principal
note.

a) Play six notes on every quarter-note (crotchet).

b)

Andante un poco adagio ($\quarternote$ = 50)

a)

Rondo
Allegretto grazioso ($\quarternote$=88)

a)

a) The octaves in this and the following measure may be
played with both hands.

PIANO SONATA
in A minor

Edited, revised and fingered by
Richard Epstein

Wolfgang Amadeus Mozart
K. 310

a)

Andante cantabile con espressione (♩= 96)

a)

a)

Presto (♩=92)

a)

PIANO SONATA
in A Major

Edited, revised and fingered by
Richard Epstein

Wolfgang Amadeus Mozart
K. 331

Tema
Andante grazioso (♪ = 120)

Var. I

Var. III (♪ = 112)

Var. V

Adagio (♪ = 60)

Var. VI

Allegro (♩ = 116)

a) The C sharp must enter with the bass note of the left hand.

Menuetto ($\bullet = 116$)

Trio

Menuetto D.C.

Alla turca
Allegretto (♩ = 126)

Rondo

a)

b) Play the first A in the bass with the C sharp in the
right hand.

a) Play the four notes in either hand simultaneously.

b)

PIANO SONATA
in C Major

Edited, revised and fingered by
Richard Epstein

Wolfgang Amadeus Mozart
K. 545

a)

Rondo

Allegretto grazioso (♩= 104)

PIANO SONATA
in A Major

Edited and with fingering by
Giuseppe Buonamici

Franz Schubert
D. 664

Allegro. ($\flat$ = 80)